Stuck in the Middle

by Jaimes Palacio

Pale Ale Poets Series

FarStarFire Press
April 2000

www.FarStarFire.com

Stuck in the Middle

Consulting Editors:

John Gardiner
John C. Harrell
Lee Mallory

Printed in The United States of America

by

FarStarFire Press
26701 Quail Creek, Suite 251
Laguna Hills, CA 92656
949.362.7499
www.FarStarFire.com
info@FarStarFire.com

"Bottled" was previously published in *Beyond the Valley of Contemporary Poets.* "Static" has been previously published in *51%.*

ISBN 1-929250-17-7

Printed in Microsoft Optimum True Type

FarStarFire Press provides a forum for uniquely sophisticated poets' voices. The Pale Ale Series is based on featured readers at the Thursday evening readings hosted by John Gardiner. Weekly readings are held at the Laguna Beach Brewing Company on Pacific Coast Highway, in Laguna Beach, California.

Dedicated to my brother, Luis, and my sister, Carmen. The express of imagination cannot begin to find the words that would describe how much you mean to me.

Table of Contents

How Many Rashomons Does it Take to Screw in a Lightbulb?

(For Arthur Paul Carmona)

1.

I have dreamt myself
a shadow in wonderland. Awake
and down the Rabbit Hole, I see
the man with the gun exiting
a local smoothie outlet. Black
cap on his head, he escapes
with $343.86 in a dented, primer-gray
pickup.

2.

Stunned witnesses vow, the possible Hispanic towered
over eight feet, was armed with a sawed-off shotgun,
possibly an Uzi, wore a black cap and shouted defiantly;
"GO AHEAD MONKEY BOYS!
PELT ME WITH YOUR DONUTS!"
as he jumped into what could have been an exact
replica of the Oscar-Meyer Wienermobile.

Evidence, however, leads to the arrest of a Hawaiian.

3.

This is how shadows deceive.

The boy, Arthur, detained at gunpoint. Witnesses confused
 until the Hawaiian's cap is brought and placed
 on Arthur's head.

Someone proclaims it : " *EVIDENCE.*"

Someone else remarks:
" *It concreted in my mind that that was him.*"

The Superior Court Judge shakes his head, mutters:
" *No trial is perfect.*"

That mad, court appointed attorney ejaculates bright,
 helpless words hovering like misguided UFOs
 or Wonder Woman's Magic Lassos.

A crowd forms. Ushers take tickets, pass out programs.
The witnesses, grinning like Kubrick's monkeys, throw
hotel keys, personal undergarments.

The Assistant District Attorney levitates, wearing
an *I'M WITH CTHULHU!* T-shirt.

The severed head of Benito Mussolini appears. I smell
old grease, sulphur,
...cranberries.

The police, raising opera glasses, accuse me of
double-parking,
ferret smuggling,
attempting the beautiful without a license.

4.

Let us pray:

GIVE US LAUGHING
NEON! SMILING
COMMERCE! HEALTH
CLUB MEMBERSHIPS!

GIVE US CLEAN COUNTERTOPS! ROMANTIC CITIES!
LUCRATIVE COCA-COLA ENDORSEMENTS!
GIVE US OUR DAILY BREAD-PEPPERED
WITH ARTIFICIAL PRESERVATIVES!
Amen

5.

Shut up! Just shut the hell up! This law is a barbed wire
lozenge! Swallow it and you'll be burning
books! This is love!
As a fist! Religion as white-
noise! This justice is rust! Nothing more
than an ignorant geek show!

6.

The crowd appears upset. I repeat, the crowd appears upset.

7.

In jail, the sobbing woman
clutches the cell-bars of the prisoner
barely glimpsed within.

On the floor there is a shattered light bulb,
the shards scattered like dead soldiers
on some cold, gray battlefield.

In each shard, a reflection-the prisoner
dissected by the scattering- here, an ear,
                                                            there, a brow,
                                                            the nose,
                                                            the chin,
                                                            an eye; wet, blinking,
                                             the mouth, tripping in response,

                                                       " No mama, I didn't do it."

   I get on my knees
     to gather the shards
       but already they're gone.

Jaimes-836

1\.
Shoplifting, but They Call It Burglary: Main Jail O.C.

A poisoned place. The air stretched
like a policeman's vocal chords caught
in mid-scream. Head dangerously tilted,
fanged, spitting and profane.

This is the big business
of justice. Held together precipitously
by chewing gum and the crushed
backs of its worker bees. The long line of men
in orange jumpsuits told to keep:

" Hands in pockets!"

" Eyes front!"

We are asked to make our shoes
sing. To be the shapes
in the holding tanks. We are given
wrist bands to define our temperature:

White: cooperative,
calm,
non-homosexual;
addicts, alcoholics, thieves

Yellow: aggressive,
problematic.

Red: violent,
anti-social;
rapists, murderers.

We are white-banders. Instructed to reply
with the last three digits of our case number.

We are separated by origin of birth. Warned:

"Do not play with the Blacks or Chinese."

On the outs
they sometimes bury the dead
by mistaken identity.

2.
Momentarily Reunited with Our Clothes, We Embrace Them Like Old Friends: First Transfer – Theo Lacy Correctional Facility

In holding, we trade
histories, race origami, belt out
show tunes and hip-hop until cuffed

We are brought two by two. Fill the bus
like wandering floodwaters. We learn:
every time we are transferred, the county pockets
one hundred and eight dollars a head.

We glimpse apparitions of strip-malls
and vaguely familiar

routines through the scrimmed windows.

Like the visions of drowning men.
We see ghosts everywhere.

3.
Here We Do Not Hoard Toilet Paper, Are Given Soap to Shower With: Second Transfer - Musick (aka, the Farm)

Ignoring each other's nudity, we suit up. It is very cold.
Our bodies stippled by the afternoon wind.

The previous owner has left a comb in one of the
pockets of my jumpsuit.
Here, the little things count most.

In the barracks, we measure time by the shifting
light. The card games in the dayroom. The television
screen jumping every time something is deemed
inappropriate.

Silence has become a *"RADIO!"*

The broken snore loudly, dreaming
of busted cam-shafts, girls refusing
to return calls, great Hammerheads
circling still waters.

4.
This Version of Purgatory Sponsored by the Redundancy Department of Redundancy Department: Arraignment - South Court

All day they monitor us.
There is even a camera strategically aimed
at the toilet.

From time to time an ethereal voice rises
from behind the thick, concrete to call out
someone.

The magazines date back to 1986.

Lunch is a sack:
A bologna sandwich. A baggie filled with lettuce
Cookies.

No drink.

Somehow my cellmates sleep.
I pace, keeping well behind the red line
and the cell bars.

5.
Time Served and I Nearly Cry in Relief.

The last bus spits us out
at Main Jail's entrance.

Free men breathing
lost air. We touch
everything

Our dancing forms illuminated
by the early morning moon
already surrendering.

It Was Strangely Reminiscent of a Party the Night Before

God
has amnesia. Sleep
is slow. Red like apples. Green
like envy.
Yes,
Eve resembled Isabella
Rosselini. This is worse
than a theory. It is a dream. Legend
has it that Eden was just a desert
strip in Texas, but with a really good
advertising budget.
Eve was the scapegoat. (It was Adam
setting his sights
with the Machlicher.)
God
was the impact.
God
was the shattering.
God
was the windshield. After the parade
the ticker tape was given
a Litmus test. The Hew bushes
were photographed and interviewed
for LIFE magazine. The diction of tongues
agitated, turned
Babel. Screaming:

"THE GARDEN IS BURNING!"

"THE PLAN HAS BEEN COMPROMISED!"

"A TEMP AGENCY HAS BEEN
RUNNING THINGS FOR YEARS!"

The next sound you hear will be extinction.
The next sound you hear will be God going blind.

Bottled

A skyline tumbles. Red embers
under a sad midnight. Pan's siren
tongue claws and buffets the bleeding sky. Faces sink
in and out of the far reaching waves of ignition.
Eyes keep score of the bluffing light. Symtex with its
constant conversation
as hunchbacked survivors pan for shelter
in the choked shade. It is 1940s London.
The Euro-Theatre casting for all able-bodied. It is fearless
Kamikaze strafings at Pearl Harbor. No regret
or panic in the windscreens of the children
of the red sun. It is the Enola Gay. Nagasaki turned sand
searching for geometry. It is Oklahoma City. It is the
running commentary of history. Allowing for Manifest
Destinies, Selective Breeding. There is always an
experiment. A sovereign plan. Hidden cannons spanning
Mediterranean seas. Okhotsk and Qingdao surrounded by
ticking waters. Guerrillas who can operate AK47s
but can't read. We are still sifting sand looking
for geometry. We are bending our arms
so far back they are breaking. We watch
the game. Looking for the runts
in the pack. Take meticulous pains to control
the deleterious genie we've unleashed. High and above
the horizon it winks, a corrupted Sun King, polishing the
Sword of Damocles. It smiles sadly. Talks of blast points
and acceptable casualties. It is always ready
for subtraction. We dream of vast spaces. Make runs
to Vegas or Tahoe. We paint our homes. Mend
our fences. Relax in the shade. Ignore the sunset
so very red.

Certain Things Get Lost in the Translation

(Dedicated to the Doomsday Clock)

This is an experiment.
The words are coded. in Pakistani
they roughly read:

DON'T SHOOT ME!
I HAVE NO MONEY!
I AM A COOKIE!

However, this, also, is in code. The code is ancient
Sumeric and requires a virgin sacrifice.
The playing of a Michael Bolton record. Skip

to the exorcism. The lake is filled with frightened
children. The street is falling in love with the farmer's
daughter.

Cats are everywhere. Holding forth in coffee shops
and cafes.
Extemporaneously speaking out on the dangers of
spontaneous combustion
and the limits of supernatural tendencies
in three month old Beagles. Cats on rooftops tricked out
in pink tutus imprinted with
Mighty Morphin Power Rangers, spinning
IKEA furniture on their heads, waving back issues of
Spin magazine,
watching Jimmy Page attempt a techno version of
GOD BLESS AMERICA.

Only it isn't really Jimmy-

just a guy who wants to be Jimmy,
who was actually Frank Sinatra,
who actually was an alien who likes Air Supply.

This is missing
time found at the back of a La Puente McDonalds.
Bound, castrated, and marinated with secret sauce.
This is waking

to find a horse's head (or traffic reports)
It can ruin your day.

And it's all true!

The monkeys have the car keys! The peaches are
forming conspiracies! They are holding for ransom: the
five missing Pensacola Tomcats! The real Shroud Of
Turin! The exact location of Area 51!
They have the missing link under wraps!
Plan to turn Atlantis
into slum housing! Valhalla into a flophouse!

They plan to bring back The Bugaloos.

This is where the exorcism fails. The ghosts bribed and
making a killing
in munitions. The children getting desperate fill graves
with dirty noise,
cigarette ash, the broken idols of their youth.

Opportunity knocks. A country we don't acknowledge
often moves

the clock's minute hand just a bit closer. Somewhere

Southwest of Los Alamos, giggling profusely, a serious
case of the munchies, genuflecting in front of some
great, magical, sacred,
Bong God. Sounding like a cross between
Jack Nicholson
and a chipmunk trapped in a blender.

It talks of peaches gone sour. Of shadows and ash.
It says:

*"Don't believe everything you trigger! Certain things get
lost in the translation! "*

It's as if Nostrodamus predicted Tupperware.
Must See T.V. Karaoke
but missed the Apocalypse. Missed the hysterical
cameos
of the Emergency Broadcast System.
A mighty scar on the face of the sky. Counting down.

Heading towards the ultimate blind date.

The Cats Hold Conspiracy Theories

Luigi focuses intently on a patch
of blank. Genetic radar has been picking up
subliminal codes:
mice,
lizards,
the occasional, unlicensed, guided missile.

He is the whiskered sentinel. The winter
coated old guard. He believes he does his job well. He
has caught
nothing all morning.

Space is something Luigi is abundantly expert at
trapping.

Actual objects give him difficulty. He has come to
believe
that most objects, (except food) are the devil's
work. He has named such objects:

"Meow."

Jackie suspects
closed doors.
This, she reasons, is surely a sign
of unhealthy activity:
Alien abductions.
Illegal DNA tampering
Cheerleader barbecues.

Black market babysitting.
Gas price gouging.
Tupperware parties.

Presidents could be vanishing! Governments toppled!
Nations ruined!
Mafia! Terrorists! Enraged postal workers! *DOGS*!

Yet the door remains doggedly mute.
Neither confirms nor denies anything as it is questioned.
Jackie sharpens her claws as Luigi strolls by, glances suspiciously,
and then leaves.

Presumably, to get back to work.

Working for the Wiz

There is no *Yellow Brick Road* .
The Wizard has long lost his teeth. Sags
in the corner suppressed.

This is *Emerald City* redefined
for the callous. In this version, Dorothy is in cahoots
with the Wicked Witch, forming a sisterhood
of sadism.

They arrive: two human wrecking balls trailed
by a small, yapping, dingy poodle. Toto
as a grotesque, spoiled harpie-child.

This most unholy of trilogies!
This gaudy, tag-team, demolition derby parade!
This venomous cabal!

So
I click my heels.
Once. Twice. Three times... Nothing!

The witch, a tacky, shimmering tornado of
olive-green eye makeup and fist-sized
purple, plastic earrings, swoops down.
Corners me.

"I hear you have been writing poetry on the company's computer."

She accuses.

"Understand this: there is to be no poetry on the company's computer!"

Suddenly I'm having evil *Crucible* flashes: stakes, fire,
Salem justice.
Death by drowning. The barbarous Queen melting
like a good sunset. Shouting it out from every hilltop:

"DING- DONG THE WITCH IS DEAD!"
(Only more creatively because this would be copyright infringement.)
Hey, unlike some folks
I don't need a house to fall on me
to know we have a severe compatibility problem here.

And over what? Words! The witch disturbed
by the fact that there was heightened language
in the company's data base! As if form and meter could
cast some grisly, emasculating spell.

Poetry running amok!
Sestinas unleashed!
Sonnets and Villanelles wild and untamed!
Haiku destroying the very fabric of mankind!
Corrupting, undermining, turning the helpless
into...
into...
poets!

No!

That sort of thing just wouldn't be copacetic.

So, with a few ignorant words a war is given birth.
I, a loyal soldier of the ironic gesture,
put my fingers to the keyboard and began
to write.

I Cartoon

In the center frame	the dropping	body conforms to the crucificial
pose; velocity,	trajectory,	adamant as stigmata. Open-
mouthed-surprised	by the dialogue	bubble escaping. Stuttering
like a careless rumor	This is	second hand smoke. How we
lost: frozen in the	missionary	position during the last ice age.
Breaking	blue and	bits of her in the technology.
Something misled	reminds me	of a warning. The cock of
a trigger waiting.	Apology	reaching like a shotgun blast-
all mighty big,	as trembling	as Chicken Little's sky. But
this different dream.	This swimming	away from sharks.
Pulled into:	*We're*	*gonna need a bigger boat!*
territory: salted	bones,	floating hubcaps, a box,
of smiling, plastic,	bunnies,	Walt Disney's corpse-
less head	lip syncing	excerpts from the Haunted Mansion.
I see my own severed	hands clapping	maniacally, passing before me.
Television screens fill	with dark teeth.	Blue Gills discuss the latest
Spielberg. Hammers	slowly	move in concentric circles.
Pool with the In	Crowd; the	gutless members of the
Chechnia	Liberation	Great Whites disperse
yellow parking	citations demand	proof of insurance. I
fumble with my	registration.	*"Look ,"* I say, *"I know*
brown eyes	*talk too much*	*I have developed a lisping*
talent	*for caricature.*	*Listen, the bruises, the echo*
of crushed stars	*and birdsong*	*spinning in a halo. This is*
the aftermath of	*drowning.*	*Being caught between a falling*
sky. Desperate	*voice attempting*	*sight above stiletto pigments.*
Ducking a tumbling	*landscape*	*Endless gray ocean, (as deep*
as any question.)"	And the	question: Why? why have you
forsaken me?	Answer coming	in coded telepathy, in waves,
in a foreign tongue,	poised with	a grin and a mallet labeled
ACME, eyeballs	protruding	classic Tex Avery,
stretching infinity,	veins popping	like subway track. I blink.
Click my Ruby	slippers.	Perform the sign of the cross.

Leave an embedded tooth; a souvenir for the next time.

Scary

TOO MANY LAURAS!
Giving me the slip.

Again.
Pink memo.

"Will you go in the back room by the answering machine and let me kiss you?"

In the back room kissing me. Candid
arms like clever sanctuaries.
Like Cinerama. Like wide
wide vistas.
(Where are the chorus girls? I gotta dance! I gotta sing!)
These funhouse tongues are tapping
secret autographs. They are humming
Tony Bennet and Sondheim. They are whispering:

"You must kill the president!"

They are making the sign of the cross. But it isn't me.
I don't go much to the theatre anymore.

It's not really Laura chatting up Ulysses. Inviting
him to a fireman's party in the hills. Not Laura trading
blades with Errol Flynn and Lawrence Harvey. Last seen
in a bowling alley distributing nude Polaroids of her
late husband. It surely must be
her Doppelganger driving the big, black Toyota
into the crowd. Singing an off-key rendition of

I KNOW WHAT BOYS LIKE.

It wasn't Laura in the back room closing her eyes.
Filling my greedy mouth.
Filling my greedy mouth.

Every Love Story Leads to Burial

Spare little attention to the choraling
boy at the foot of your balcony
his is the battered old song of whales
missing the sea

He came to this stage dragging
his words like reluctant bait
across the microphones of the world
eyes sharp with white convictions he sang

While thousands died trapped
in falling castles
his ego became aria bellowed
for the film rights

Felons were taught Soft Shoe
aliens visited the Vatican
in the tittering wreckage
of youth you were spotted

Skipping rope wearing time
as an excuse
under the parking lights your blue eyes said:

"Your love is like a shotgun blast caught in Pekinpagh's slow motion."

He began a habit
of rushing into collapsing buildings

Lips sewn together eyes filling
with salt

He pushes at the coffin's lid
drowns stamping at spiders,
you legally have your last name changed
move to a trailer park

become closer
to God.

When We Close Our Eyes

After midnight
the hypnotic metronome
of the windshield wipers coaxes
my eyes to sleep. Uncontrolled, the wheels
slip.

Mother is there. Bruised and incoherent. Gambling
saviors for cocktails. She lays
a photo album before her like an open casket. Turns
the pages, slowly filling the grave over
and over again.

In a scrapbook there are pictures
of you. Candid postures focus
on the length of your smile, the confident brightness
of your eyes. I can trace the progression
of hairstyles. Define each year by the colors.
Or the lovers, friends we have brushed past-fortunate
to be recorded in the act of submission.

PAY ATTENTION.

These are clues. Hinted
symptoms and whispers.

I have fallen. I am in love with you.

It's a stupid thing. These inferior movements hardly
could reach you.

Yet, I cluck. Pretend and put on a blind dumb show.
Close my eyes and fill the unrequited silences
in the middle of the night.

Just so many graves before the neck snaps
eyelids open like pages in a photo album. Turning
the wheels back. The city's skyline trembling.
A ghost ship, tall and spectral
in the mist.

The Random Big Show

Is this the way it will end? Rush hour. The camera hovering.
KFI and "*News every hour, on the half and when it breaks.*"
Blue cars. White cars. An exterminating truck with a cartoon rat.
Incrementally creeping. Profane and prickly.
Palms. Fingers. Vibrating glass. Keep the coal from eyes
as recycled martyrs wince on faded dashboard skins.

THIS IS A PUBLIC SERVICE ANNOUNCEMENT! The skin
of truth is a subtle heretic; a raging Prometheus stuck on the
cloverleaf.
PAY ATTENTION TO THE DETAILS: the color of his eyes.
The stains on the white, hunched palms. The broken
flirting vampires of his teeth. The way he stabs the radio. Picks
a station. Rations
the information. Judges the music. The maze has followed the
rats-
gridlocked pilgrims trapped in miles of seething, metal skins.

TRUE OR FALSE: *Don Quixote battled windmills with a
toothpick.*
*The Apocalypse will be a choreographed, over budgeted
affair available on Pay-Per-View. The Anti-Christ will breakfast
at McDonalds. Will have blue* eyes.

Will have kind blue, eyes.

The maze has swallowed the rats.
The demographics broken
down into common victims: steel, bone, skin.
The grading has no curve. The over reaching
dialogues, the costumes picked
only signify a transient pose; the hesitant pulls and pricks
of shifting favor.

TRUE OR FALSE: *You must pluck out your eyes*
if: They are blue. Your lover has proclaimed it over.
You have fallen in love with intangibles. It promotes high ratings.
It is Saigon,
1973. It is Mogadishu, 1965. It is Bokaroke,

1951. It is a wing and a prayer and promises broken.
Broken...A scant few miles from Pickfair
the Hollywood sign fades in it's humbled skin.
From high above, not even a bird's eye
can pinpoint the rats
nesting in the rafters.
Scuttling back and forth, ducking for cover.

Visible sins are not always explained by the camera's eye.
It can only report on the breaking movements, blossoms
picked
from rat's teeth. The shotgun. The bodies. The car, on fire,
overturned.

Psycho Notes from a Traffic Jam

or

Gridlock Epiphany Rant

Note: in an effort towards politeness the following piece has been edited by the author. Certain expletives have been replaced with randomly chosen household appliances.

Dirty blue
Pinto votes
Pro-life.

Forest green
Microbus swerves
righteously. Claims to know
when Christ is coming back.

Bright red
El Camino blinks.
Smiles
"GOD LOVES YOU!"

There seems to be a trend here.

And as the faded, yellow Cavalier
filled with barking Germans
passes- a guitar's neck attempting Flamenco, caught
wagging through the window,
the sadness of frustration leaps at the jugular of the man
in the dented Crème Honda.

The sun presses, presses, presses
glass. Heat terrorism in sweat filled refrains.
These cars. This mob. Blocking his path.

His path.

Tense. Tight. Tired. Face contorting. Growling.
Morphing.
Demon-God-Manic-Driver!

"I DON'T BELIEVE THIS!"
(Stated to no one who could listen.)
Mud words bursting
lips. A carnivore's roar!

"GOURMET FONDUE CROCK!
GOURMET FONDUE CROCK!
GOURMET FONDUE CROCK!"

It cries.

"FURNACE ME! FURNACE ME! FURNACE ME!"

It cries.

"FURNACE-ME-GOURMET-FONDUE-CROCK-FURNACE-
ME-WITH-A-40-FOOT-REPLICA-
OF-ANN-MARGRET-IN-BYE-BYE-BIRDIE-
WAVING-A-GLASS-SPIKED-DILL-PICKLE-MAKER!"

It felt compelled to add
illogically.
And this man: a prickly, profane monster reawakened!

Stubbly, demented, child-king, road warrior!
Spouting maniacally. Hatching from this fever!
This need to scream his rampaging Braille
deep into the hot asphalt!
To rev his engines like a good Bruce Springsteen song
and just soar over the orange hatted off-ramps!
The construction clouding his vision!
The screeching kids craning their necks
in the gray Buick station wagon festooned with
YES ON 22 decals.

But there is a trend here
and the last vestiges of civility disappear
as a big, brown, Chevy pick-up, sporting gun racks
and *VOTE DORNAN !* bumper stickers, cuts him off,
giving him the finger.

"STUPID-MOTHER-FURNACE-COMPUTER-
DISHWASHER-BASTER-SON-OF-A-FURNACE-
MONKEY-BUTT-LOVIN-GOURMET-FONDUE-CROCK...
DORKHEAD!"

Swinging at the air in baboon-like mating ritual.
An insane,
Turret-Syndromed faucet of a man. Slipping.

Falling.

The final phase. Complete. Total. Imbecility.

Futile efforts at speech arrive bruised.
Bewildered:

"YEEK! FLOOP! GIRK! DASK!"

An alien language from some mightily confused galaxy.
Storm wracked processes failing.
Failing. No release. No escape.

The wind bringing smoke. The stench
of scorched oil.

The man transformed oblivious
to the fact that this is a moment
of inheritance.

In the Midst of Flight They Forget

(Why Prince of Egypt disappointed)

Parting
seas! Evil
swarms! Black
plagues!
Oh yes!

It's a musical.

Moses played by Batman.
(It's the staff-chicks did the staff!)
Catwoman appears to quote
the Kama Sutra.
The third row man notes:
"Ghandi didn't write the Kama Sutra..."

Oceans migrate! Tides shift! The burning bush speaks

Ebonics!

When will you believe?

First born are taken-thrown
into car commercials, product placement. The
Hollywood sign is butchered,
passed out to the drowning
masses. Mount Arrarat is auctioned off
in parcels on the Net. The winds of change whisper:

"Mariah..."

Oh, sweet Mariah!
Gives us her all!
Gives us a climax
every time!
Gives us Hollywood!
(As produced by Vegas.) Bubble gum
culture Manna cascades from Saffron painted skies.
(But it's $7.50 a pop
and doesn't include parking.)
We stand dripping
in lambs blood as corporate spirits pass
above advertising the latest in teenage
footwear. We raise strangled hands. Shout
hoarsely to broken nosed Gods:

"LET MY PEOPLE GO! "
"KLATU-BARATA-NICTO!"
"NIKE. JUST DO IT."

Hey, we are promised
some lovely violence: the head of Cole Porter.
His thin, piano fingers kicking and screaming
from a sampling board! The Gershwins fed
to the MGM lion! Over the Rainbow recast
in a woman's prison,
a girl's locker room,
a mud pit with two chesty strippers glinting
like beached, miracle fish in Galilee.

Hollywood is ready
for its close up. Demands disco, funk, Busby Berkely
tricked
up in trip-hop.

Oh, save a prayer
for the lizard tongued acolytes sacrificing sun flower
faced ingenues
to Backstreet Boys' demographics!

Save a prayer for the machines grinding
our breath.

Save a prayer for the common
denominator. The trivial
pursuit.

The romantically tragic spreading
honeyed palms. Singing:
Hosanna! Hosanna in the highest!

There We Are...

(For Paul Tatum)

January 22, 1998, Beverly Hills Hilton
14th Annual Hotel Association Awards
Martin Mull, M.C.
Buzz Aldrin, Keynote Speaker.

Did you know that Charles Hurwitz
is cutting down the last Redwoods?

(You think of the strangest things when you're bored.)

Just hours
before they held
the 55th Golden Globe Awards
in this very room. Now
I shine
a spotlight on a man who walked on the moon.

Like any good tourist
he has brought his personal slides.
Points to them and says
that in less than 10 years
it will actually be feasible to build hotels
in space.

And someone once said:
History can make us richer or it can deem
us insignificant.

And I remembered. Remembered the news
paper talking. Talking about the man found
dead near a Russian train station, where he was rushing
to meet an anxious caller. Such blue
eyes. No make that brown eyes. No make that green
eyes. He was shot in the head,
the spine,
the chest.

Blame fell:
    a fanatic obsessed with a child star,
    a cult expecting spacecraft (who found the sun,)
    the Chechnia Liberation,
    the CIA,
    a corrupt Russian mayor,
        (who just wanted the real estate)
    a powerful hotel cartel in collusion with investors,
    with the KGB,
    the FBI,
    the Prime Minister,
    the Dali Lama,
    the Muppets,
    the missing
    link,
    the possibilities:

    History can make us richer!

I think:
    bottom line.
I think:
    Location.
    Location.
    Location.

Fractals

Undone by Cupid's pipe bomb,
Lancelot has a dream; trembling
like John Wilkes Booth's gun.

Or that big, anonymous, speeding car subtracting
the girl scout
at the crosswalk.

Guinevere is on the scene. She's heard shots.
Hired assassins pull Excaliber free from
stuttering fists.
They say: *"Here are the questions. "*
They say: *"Factor in the variables. "*
They say: *"Solve for Y."*

Why.
This is the new math. The black
knight funnels millions. Believes his children
are untraceable.
Believes in the crucifixion
of the baby
Jesus.

The P.T.A. at the gates of Ragnarok carry banners:

"SAVE OUR CITIES!"

Camelot has fallen
to the Vandals! Merlin grafittees

in bold, pink neon. Across a dozen
universes the new math is tabulated,
counted...

1.

"THAT IDIOT CUT ME OFF! "

This is how Morganna handles traffic.
Privately wishing
she hadn't given up the voodoo. (But damn!
It was fattening!)

These days she is sleek. These days
she tastes like Vanilla.
These days she is more enigma.
These days the general
public knows:
She had joined a cult of fervent Hari-Krishnas.
She had left to start a holy order
of dyslexic vegetarians.
She was secretly an Amway product
salesperson.
She had been recruited by the CIA
to command a tribe
of Leftist, Peruvian feminists.
She had, tragically, gone into banking.

These days no one knows anything.
These days numbers hold little magic.

2.

Guinevere imagines spectator voices moving past
his death.

(Misdirected as his grails proved.)

She cries in tongues. Prepares
his tomb
with perfume and lipstick. The voices, finding teeth,
whisper
his infidelity.

3.

Mordred's mouth fills
with shrapnel. He misunderstood
her scared enchantment.
Her lovely California
legs spread-eagled
on the operating table. Removing
the Algebra of his delinquent
Geometry. Her eyes turning
Dorothy, but that's another
story.

4.

Merlin now runs
a Karaoke bar.   Stoned

secretary banshees.
An impotent Elvis. Gyrating
cowboys dropping plastic,
hustling the schoolgirls barking
their dangerous age.
Merlin recognizes
the nuclear picture.
Rockwell gone
Go-Go and absurd.   On stage
Celine Dion gives
birth
to Cthlhu's son. Packaged
for optimum multiplicity,
Up-to-Date-Pulse-Pound-Glamour-Hipster
silently erases
the unfashionable. Notes:

"They kill dinosaurs in these parts."

Merlin stabs
at his watch. 10 minutes
till midnight
and a long way home.

5.

This constant bartering I am expected
to be proficient at!
This begging, corrupted, flailing compromise!
This shallow purpose! Oh, I can play the fool with
exquisite manufacture!
I can bellow with perfect timing! I can rage! Wash myself

in glamorous pretense! Yet, in this-this
course and bloodless tune;
this apology painting itself in impossible colors,
too bright to wear, too sharp to salvage! And what value
do we give to explain the sweat in the palms of the dying
common man? The boy caught in another's definition
of honor? Who, even as he pales and shudders raises
his small fists in defiance and screams: "I will not be this
stupid, handsome corpse!"

It is a play on words. It is a play of words. It is a play.
Arthur leaves the stage to tremendous applause.

6.

They found the lady
in the lake. Face down
Purple and unrecognized.
Her features no longer mathematically
proportionate for the 18-30 demographics.
The slow, cold dialogue
of her suicide like white
noise turning
channels

7.

The results are totaled. The solutions reached.
At the funeral, the family stands calcified in grief.
Somewhere
else,

stuck in the middle
between a father's sins
              and a mother's bitter defeat
Lancelot continues to dream
slowly dying in the convenience store parking lot.
The point of entrance just above
the right eyebrow.

Lancelot continues to dream
and
with his last breath

his hand
falls,

forms
into
a
fist.

Static

(For Taylor-Mari)

She was a child raised on the never ending promise
of Armageddon.
The ashen girl watching the dancing
couples on the ceiling,
barely following the cracks in the glass.

I am the ghost at the funeral. Hovering over my brother
at his daughter's casket. Others carry the burning
documents, casually explain where we go when we die.
Married friends sincerely point out the choices and:

"Which one is it going to be?"

Mother, praying to deaf saviors, drinks Martinis
straight from a can, stumbles in the aisles.

Taylor-Mari began in a moment of unfettered charity.
Given a machine to massage the chrome in her eyes,
the mercury in her lungs.
A plastic tube to feed her
suffocation.

Now I am the flowers at the grave; incongruous,
necessary.

She took in the inferior puppet show seeking something
worthier
than the spine of slow midnight. The stuttering

blood of radiation. She becomes blue-eyed history.
Becomes memory.

Her fading
poisoned suit, clutching at quicksand
futures, navigating sand
papered halls.

Now, I am static.
(The way I build conversation in this place.)
She and her broken fingers. Walking away slowly with a
sigh.
I am just a survivor.

She is now
light.

Acknowledgments:

The author wishes to thank Victor and Lea for their leaps of faith, food, teaching and woozles. Thanks also to Bil and Carole for their passion and compassion. Charles and Phish for their accumulated brilliance; the shadow of their steps one could never fill. Nancy and Kevin for the karaoke, Jamba Juice; a home away from home.

Special thanks to all who have supported the Java Garden, Gypsy Den, Laguna Beach Brewing Company, Riverside and Valley Contemporary Poets readings - especially Mary and Nick and Beth and Chris for their friendship and encouragement.

Back cover photograph courtesy of Carrie Piela

FarStarFire Press is publishing thematic poetry of all kinds. Our publications present works suitable for any audience of any age. We are proud to offer the following titles:

- *Upside Brown*: by Derrick Brown — Jan 99
- *The Blue Book Poems*: by Carole Luther — Feb 99
- *Traildust*: by John Gardiner — Mar 99
- *Beaches Vol. 1 and Vol. 2*: by Bil Luther — Apr 99
- *For Lori*: by Daniel McGinn — May 99
- *Girltalk*: by Katya Giritsky — Jun 99
- *The 1999 Laguna Beach, CA Slam Team* — Jul 99
- *Borrowing Li Po's Moon*: by John C. Harrell — Aug 99
- *Fruit On My Lips*: by J.D. Glasscock — Sep 99
- *The Dark Beyond the Stars*: by Cassandra Hill — Oct 99
- *Learning to Speak*: by Victor D. Infante — Nov 99
- *You Make the Balloons, I'll Blow Them Up*: by Paul Suntup — Dec 99
- *Two Sides Now:* by Misty Mallory & Lee Mallory — Dec 25, 99
- *Scream!*: by Bil Luther — Jan 00
- *Season of the River*: by Lawrence Schulz — Feb 00
- *Trusting the Moon*: by John Gardiner — Mar 00

Future Publications to Include:

- The Tao Te Ch'ang: a multimedia CD by Jim Fontana, Bil Luther and Carole Luther.
- Twenty Years: a multimedia CD version of John Harrell's print work with Moki Martin, artist.
- Tao and Zen Wilderness: a multimedia CD by John Gardiner, Carole and Bil Luther.

We can be contacted by email at info@farstarfire.com.

FarStarFire Press
26701 Quail Creek, Suite 251
Laguna Hills, CA 92656
949.362.7499
http://www.farstarfire.com